THE LEICESTERSHIRE
& RUTLAND
COLOURING BOOK

First published 2017

The History Press
The Mill, Brimscombe Port
Stroud, Gloucestershire, GL5 2QG
www.thehistorypress.co.uk

British Library Cataloguing in Publication Data.
A catalogue record for this book is available from the British Library.

ISBN 978 0 7509 7889 7

Typesetting and origination by The History Press
Printed and bound in Great Britain by TJ International Ltd.

THE LEICESTERSHIRE & RUTLAND

COLOURING BOOK

PAST AND PRESENT

Take some time out of your busy life to relax and unwind with this feel-good colouring book designed for everyone who loves Leicestershire and Rutland.

Absorb yourself in the simple action of colouring in the scenes and settings from around the county, past and present. From iconic architecture to picturesque vistas, you are sure to find some of your favourite locations waiting to be transformed with a splash of colour.

There are no rules – choose any page and any choice of colouring pens or pencils you like to create your own unique, colourful and creative illustrations.

Earthwork's Florist, Uppingham ▸

King Power Stadium, Leicester ▸

Rutland County Museum, Oakham ▶

A river flows through Burbage Woods, Hinckley ▸

Bosworth Battlefield Heritage Centre, Sutton Cheney ▸

Melton Carnegie Museum, Melton Mowbray ▸

Rutland Water, Oakham ▶

Wistow Maze, Wistow ▸

Charnwood Museum, Loughborough ▸

A Leicester Corporation tram on East Park Road, Leicester, *c.* 1916 ▶

Ashby-de-la-Zouch Castle ▶

Foxton Locks, near Market Harborough ▶

Blackburn Buccaneer, Bruntingthorpe Air Museum ▸

Kirby Muxloe Castle ▶

Market Harborough ▸

The 1620s House and Garden at Donington le Heath ▸

The University of Leicester ▶

New Walk Museum and Art Gallery, Leicester ▸

Platform at Great Central Railway, Loughborough ▸

Stoneywell in Ulverscroft was designed by Ernest Gimson, one of the most influential figures of the British Arts & Crafts Movement ▸

Leicester Cathedral ▶

Leicester Guildhall ▸

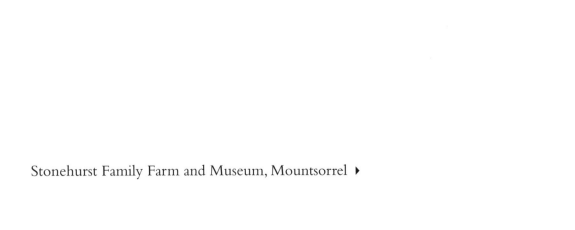

Stonehurst Family Farm and Museum, Mountsorrel ▸

Old John Tower, Bradgate Park, Leicester ▶

The ruins of Leicester Abbey in Abbey Park, Leicester ▸

Hinckley Fire Brigade, 1930s ▸

Rockingham Castle, Market Harborough ▸

Melton Mowbray pork pie ▶

Ashby-de-la-Zouch Canal, Market Bosworth ▸

The National Space Centre, Leicester ▶

Archaeological dig at Greyfriars car park, Leicester, in
2012, where the burial place of Richard III was found ▸

The Leicestershire and Rutland Wildlife Trust manages thirty-five reserves to protect and enhance wildlife and wild places ▶

High Street, Leicester, *c.* 1960 ▸

Leicester City Market ▶

Charnwood Forest alpacas, Loughborough ▸

Barnsdale Gardens, Oakham ▸

Oakham Castle ▶

Church Street, Lutterworth, *c.* 1906 ▸

Historic quarry trains and diggers can be seen at Rocks by Rail and the Living Ironstone Museum in Cottesmore ▸

Market Bosworth Country Park ▶

Donington Hall, Castle Donington ▸

The Buttercross, Oakham ▶

Tolethorpe Hall, Little Casterton, Rutland ▸

Church Street, Melton Mowbray ▸

Belvoir Castle, Grantham ▶